Landeg White was born in south Wales and has reached Portugal by way of Trinidad, Malawi, Sierra Leone, Zambia and York. Among his books are studies of VS Naipaul; of Mozambican and Malawian history; and of southern African praise poetry, along with six collections of poetry including *Where the Angolans are Playing Football* (Parthian, 2003). His translation of Camões's *The Lusiads* won the Texeira Gomes prize for 1998. He teaches at Portugal's Universidade Aberta (Open University) and is working on a translation of Camões's lyrical poems and on a biography of John Gabriel Stedman. For more information visit www.landegwhite.com.

Arab Work

Arab Work

Landeg White

PARTHIAN

Parthian
The Old Surgery
Napier Street
Cardigan
SA43 1ED

www.parthianbooks.co.uk

First published in 2006

ISBN 1-905762-01-1
978-1905762-01-9

Cover design by Marc Jennings
Inner design by books@lloydrobson.com
Printed and bound by Dinefwr Press, Llandybïe, Wales

Published with the financial support of the Welsh Books Council

British Library Cataloguing in Publication Data
A cataloguing record for this book is available from the British Library

For
Carapinheira
where I've purchase

(*Carapinheira*, village near Mafra, Portugal; variety of pear tree that gives very juicy fruit; having crisp, curled hair, hence *carapinha* – girl of mixed-descent, Moçambique)

Contents

Purchase

So I come again to design a garden
with more space than I know how to fill.
Poetry, even the translated epic's no
match for the puppy from the next allotment's
outrage at my furrow-skipping shoes.
I scratch his ears and pronounce *Bom dia*
to its quizzical owner and barrel-shaped wife.
'Are you coming to live?' I tell them, *sim*.
'To plant vegetables?' 'Fruits.' They gesture
to their grove of golden citrus. 'Your place
is full of rabbits.' And so we begin.
                                                An acre,
more or – 'Less,' contends Alice (whose
husband-less grandmother hoed each rains
four hectares, living by such husbandry).
Back at the *armazem*, she protests
at my raincoat. 'There was a puppy,'
                                                I explain.
Armazem, or *barracão*, cobwebbed roof,
serviceable walls. A fortnight after we've
bought it, the agent locates the keys.
We descend into a gloom of bat-droppings,
barrels, two hundred bottles, a wine-press
a pruning hook, a torch by way of w.c.
The pan-tiles are a starlit sky. I make
swipes with a rusty sickle. But candles,
a good spot to see out the millennium. His
bunk, whoever he was, is here. His mirror
                                                        reflects me.

My Latest Journey

My latest journey to the city
takes 50 minutes and 100 years.
I start out across a field, and wait
at the bus stop by the junction store
with women travelling to market
and old men going nowhere,

and we descend, even in August,
into a greenery so profound
the plunge annihilates all thought
this ride could have an end,
till the old men raise their hats
at the cemetery to their friends,

then each delays us, negotiating
the coach's narrow exit,
separately manipulating
hip, knee or humped back
the members that adumbrate
they're still among the quick.

The women take their elbows
clucking with motherly concern,
rewarded by a formal bow
from each gallant in his turn.
The automatic door hisses
behind them on its piston.

Then it's the *via rapida*,
the half full bus half my age,
and the emblematic barrier
of a stony mountain ridge

between here and the city where
we pretend to a monthly wage.

The girls look like sisters
with delicate cheek bones,
and high-waisted trousers
with enigmatic chains;
like auto-palm readers
they study their mobile phones.

The men are less disguisable,
more obviously their fathers'
sons in suits, more individual,
tolerant of the stranger
absorbed in his foreign journal,
and unimpressed by rumour.

I stare down from the motorway
at what we've left behind,
villages deep in the twisting valley,
anciently confined,
shaped by the land's fertility,
not by a turn of mind,

for there's nothing up here, not
even a windmill, just scrub
and abandoned quarries. Hermit
territory once perhaps,
or a *basse terre* for bandits,
but I can make out ships

in the estuary, and the towers
of the city's suspension
bridge. Consumers
loom, with a quickening
of interest, as the bus
tilts and the new horizon's

a jagged ring of apartment
blocks patrolling the moors,
forbidding as ancient
megaliths, or survivors
of a nuclear blast, painted
as we descend closer

pink and turquoise and curry
yellows, no flowering
in balconies or weathered
stone for those here
to rise up in the world,
entombed on the 10th floor.

For the heart of the city's
on, beyond the jammed
viaduct, the ring road supermarkets,
beyond the latest stadium,
where something's played out,
older than the millennium,

younger than the last CD shop
perched, sublimely ignorant,
on the ultimate outcrop
of this many-layered settlement.

Appropriately, we stop,
where the metro first descends,

tunnelling through history
to our individual stations,
my fellow villagers and I,
through pre-Roman foundations,
Visigothic debris,
Moorish irrigations,

the Crusaders' rubble,
the Navigators' bricolage,
the earthquake's upheaval,
all that to emerge
at this pre-industrial level
of a post-industrial age,

for the city's trend
is linear, with arrival
endlessly postponed.
First person plural,
this journey's end
a recurring trick of style.

The Brown Girl

When on the molasses barge, reading Austen's
Orgulho e Preconceito, she was even then,
in the swamplands, plotting houses on envelopes,

Reader, we begin this poem a long way
back, with the brown girl, just twenty-one,
on a flooded tributary of the green Zambesi,

sketching rooms for family, for sleeping
and cooking, and a hatchet-hewn
fig wood table, seating not less than twenty,

steaming upriver, the reed plumes
whitening at dawn. Motionless, the current
slides, duckweed debris spinning

in a long room with a ceiling fan and wooden
shutters, a veranda with anthuriums
in milk tins, a treadle Singer humming,

in the black eddies. The river coils
back on itself. A hippo surfaces,
yawning like a piano. Acres of lilies undulate

at the head of a flamingo estuary,
with some land like her mother's rice farm
somewhere. Thirty years on her loveliness

as the barge blunders on sunrise, a dugout
on the gold inlet, a net swirls and is cast,
while over their water pots, bra-less women

no longer blank, she is flawed with beauty.
Such things are hardly to be written of
– like the offering of beer and maize flour,

semaphore to the bargemen their satiric
invitations, as she turns the page, prettily
incensed by Darcy's too proud proposal.

the pumpkin leaves with coconut, she
pledges in this foreign corner, hallowing
in her mother's name, this plot before she builds.

Casa Uhuru

Flywell Ntima of that forgotten generation
for whom Pan Africanism would redeem
the world, has brought his wound
to a small estate, here in the Alentejo,

and stubbornly named it *Casa Uhuru*.
We have much in common, he and I, though
the same history scuppered my chances
of being a kindly DC on perpetual safari,

or a folklore crazed missionary. Our journeys
have brought us to plots in Portugal
in a pretence of putting down roots where race
is not too much of an issue. Our difference

lies in his greater ambition – viz., the flecked
bamboo he smuggled from the Ivory Coast
and watches like a nurse, or the evening
his French wife phoned him in Nairobi

to say the fever tree was in fresh shoot, and he
spent the whole night tossing in excitement.
As for his baobabs, he has three in pots,
stunted like bonsai, but in tiny leaf.

Imagine a savannah trembling with thorn trees,
a black mountain, cut by a highway,
where the poor have access and the educated prosper.
His *Casa Uhuru*'s a dream this dreamer's lost.

A Thing about Fig Trees

A thing not widely known about fig trees
is that when, come March, dove-like

leaves alight on the tips
of each rubbery twig, flapping

their wings to keep their balance,
two incorrigible green knobs

already cohabit each perch. When
it's May, and the trefoils are dark-veined,

there is indeed a whiff of the sacred
('Who told thee that thou wast naked?').

But these veils seem extrinsic
to a tree irrepressibly priapic.

Was it for this the second Adam,
riding at Passover into Jerusalem

cursed you for being fruitless, when
like his donkey you were all too visibly pagan?

For had this happened in November
when fig trees wield their knobkerries

like forests of Zulu impi,
might he have stooped to shock and awe?

Those little punch bags won't be denied
(and Jerusalem fell, as he prophesied)

Arab Work

Alice is designing a water garden
at the foot of the slope in the swamp
under the plum tree, with Easter
lilies and six types of melon. But,
it turns on a blocked waterway,
easily reverted to its proper course
– too late, though, for the plum
that in its death throes hurls
me as I climb to prune it.

Now the land's harrowed, I
recognise for the first time
what I've unseen five times:
the stone trough, the square
stone culvert, smooth as an egg,
tunneling our plot to the arched
exit. This is Arab work, a well-
watered platform raised a thousand
years back at the valley's head,

and my unfolding luck's to have
purchase where the husbandry
of a millennium still holds.
The olive trees are archives,
the soil clinging to my shoes
has been turned so many centuries
by tools that have kept their
shape and muscle. My sudden
prayer is serious: to be worthy.

Melting-Pot

The delights of a mixed-marriage! She
hoists a hoe, I heel a spade, but here's

no word for calling a spade a spade.
I decline the shoulderless tin shovel

they proffer me, ('um pã', they call it.
'Umpa, umpa,' I practice, humming Elgar's

Cockaigne), and to buy what's what
must descend to the Princess Di Emporium

declaring, whenever I plant a tree
(round peg, admirably square hole),

I'm a bife *from above the hoe-line,*
beyond the olive and cork oak line

where wives are frigid and cuisine
never penetrates, where we drink

warm beer at silly-mid-on, and bury
our dead in churchyards, and where

(spades being trumped) *my*
deadliest insult founders: to my

'You Bastard!' your *under-the-belt*
body blow hisses 'Cuckold!'

– though being as I am snow-bound,
embracing the dusky south,

how then explain she lusts for
not you, my pork-and-cheese *senhor*,

but tea on a Tennysonian
lawn barricaded with roses?

Oldest Inhabitant

Take the case of Ibne Mucana al-Isbuni,
magistrate, courtier, and Iberian humanist
('*a glass of good wine sets you up for*
Friday's prayers'). He served in Seville
at the court of the Abbadides, and afterwards
with the Zirides in Grenada. So fashioned
were his tropes ('*Regard us well, lord,*
for our brilliance is to burnish your light,
that light which descends from the Lord
of Creation') Prince Idris ordered the veil
withdrawn to gaze on the poet's face.

We meet him, sickle in hand, extemporising
satires on the barren soil of the village
of his birth ('*and if the corn exceeds*
twenty bags, armies of wild boars descend
from the wilderness of Sintra mountain').
He has abandoned processing with kings
in their finery to harvest thorns, but his thoughts
are of freedom ('*A man of purpose needs*
a windmill, turning with the clouds').
At this nine centuries' distance, it seems
a well rounded life, the journey up

and outwards, the peak, the homecoming
to a known place, a familiar calendar, where
planting begins with the swallows' flight,
windfall oranges roll among hoop-petticoat
daffodils, and each April brings drought
and the husbanding of water. So much
is evidence. For the rest, from the north
iron-clad Christians, from the Sahara

the Almoravids marched. The complete
poet, the courtier-peasant of my imaginings
vanished, save his word play and sickle.

Our Concrete Doggerel

Our quarter-built house disturbs. What
are we projecting on this vineyard?

The *armazem*'s walls and broken tiles
and wine-trough are in-fill

rubble for the concrete platform
we take our measure down from

as suddenly the Atlantic crests
above Antonio's pine forest.

With these pillars, the land
feels surveyed, diminished.

I am less in awe of its history,
its thousand years' husbandry.

Is our concrete achievement
to be planting this monument

where the wine grapes were table sweet
as the roots went down 20 feet,

and the watercourse's signature
is older than Chaucer's?

I shall work in the city
or at home through the internet,

no glib analogy drawn
between my Saxon spade and my pen,

labouring to inspire my muse,
squiring summer barbecues,

hoping against charity we are the last
to intrude on this forest's

margin, and that our upwardly-mobile peasant neighbours
with their mini-tractors and lethal crop-sprayers

will tolerate our presence
and consolidate their inheritance

with each turnip-cum-potato year,
as our concrete doggerel ends here.

Before the Oranges have Fallen

Bonfire, good fire (Johnson, 1755),
not hell's torment, nor the Inquisition's
auto-da-fé, nor England's yearly

carbonisation of Guy, but benign,
necessary flames. Prune, and burn
before planting, ash for the soil

and pleasure for the soul. On a crisp
afternoon, with an Atlantic view,
and a robin inspecting sawn-off

lichens, as my smoke's shadow
purples the up-turned earth,
I am feeding a fire, with plum

and apple prunings. This
isn't Tyger, nor Hopkins' forge,
nor Eliot's dove with the flickering

tongue descending in damnation,
nor am I priest nor presbyter
consummating the millennium, just

a man greying with average wisdom,
glad that spring comes early here
before the oranges have fallen,

ignorant of any need to make
poetry of the fact I love
lighting and tending a bon fire.

Revisiting Grasmere

There was a time the English read Wordsworth
with delight and instruction, plummeting
depths in themselves and patterns
in their understanding
of work and time and love given,
but who reads poetry now,
or can pronounce
from the century just past
two hundred lines by heart?
Our most intimate art
mislaid its audience.

There's a sort of finch settles
late afternoon on the telephone wire
a dozen feet from my veranda
and blasts away at me, shrill
as an Irish fiddle and as tuneless:
what he's about I've no idea.
Or the woodpecker
with the scarlet poll,
drilling away at the creosote pole
as though it were still a tree,
what are his Black and Decker
lobotomies to me?

Line breaks, for example,
that elementary mark of verse,
visible at twenty paces
whatever the language or competence,
how did the lack of imagination's pressure
for the turn to occur at just
that point

come, like the absence of rhyme,
to be called reform?

Today, raking mown
meadow flowers for the autumn
bonfire, I frightened a tiny
wriggling snake and close by
a baby weasel. Does
our plot connect them?
The snake slid like a boot lace
down a crack in the summer
crust. The needle-toothed
perfection I cremated.

The *canna* burns with rifle shots
and little diapason sighs;
the ivy flares like linoleum.

Yet in any airport or shopping mall, any coach
or hotel or motorway toilet, even on beaches and our
voyage to the source of the Golden River,
the young's crude quatrains
boom,

Boom,
Let's go back to my room,
We can do it all night,
Make me feel all right-

they're classics,
idols, legends to their face, their self-
belief baffles irony, their rhymes
are in deepest space, instinct
in tune with the void.

These swallows milling like termites
in the indigo glow of dusk
scream too, clicking
in their African dialects.
What makes me, so out of touch
with the times, feel
there's knowledge there, if only
I could glean it? They have
come so far, they're so
excellent at what they do,
scudding and scything
with such thrilling grace
as though meaning were not an issue.

To create the taste
you would be judged by,
to mirror the complexity of the times,
to bring all life within compass,
to discipline emotion's squadrons,
words strictly at attention,
to create the exact, unsullied
image, to shock, expose,
bewilder, fool,
look in thy heart and write,
fool, look in your heart,
the foul second-hand shop, where
boom-boom the poem starts.

These storm clouds, scudding across
the night sky over the heaving
Atlantic, are not so black
as the one pine tree

silhouetted where our garden drops.
Night, but I can find my way
to its chequered bark
blindfold. After day's particulars,
night reminds us how we hang in space,
squandering our inheritance,
more than ever dependent
on its necessary companion
art – to cut the diamond metaphor,
ridicule all courtiers, burnish
the other in ourselves, praising
the guerrilla warfare of flowers.

In this late October gale
the sickle moon is intermittent:
anchored planets and hurtling stars
gleam, and go out, and radiate again.

Mightier than, etc

For Senhor João Fonseca Gil Vincent,
his bulldozer's a precision instrument.

He could smash that 200 year olive bole
with a single uppercut, and does the inevitable,

but he prefers a featherlite dusting, a neat
filleting of culverts and driveways, that

depends on exact poise, viz., four
pile-driving telescopes opening at singular

angles to calibrated levels
(the millstone tyres revolving

uselessly) so the contraption rears
like a monster cockroach, and our senhor

with his gap-toothed digger
and a battery of levers

pats and smooths and nudges and prods
his boulders and clods

as though icing a cake,
or planting a mosaic,

or crafting a more elegant lyric
than these elephant-foot iambics,

– for as he watches the writer
watching the constructor

there's detectable irony
in his reined-in delicacy.

The mightier pen,
the sword into ploughshare,

hardly seem options
when it's ballpoint and bulldozer.

A Thing about Wrens

A thing not widely known about wrens
is that the male, before February's done,

builds three or four different nests to display
like an estate-agent to prospective Jennies

and if one clicks, he gets off with her.
This explains the behaviour

we've been jointly ogling
like gossips through the bedroom curtain,

viz., why there was no conjugal action for so long
beyond the glorious reveille of that song.

We guess she dropped by: *I like the garden*,
complimenting our birthday jasmine,

but the interior needs fixing, which
is why he flew in with the extra lichen,

and sang more fiercely, and this time scored.
As for the nests not owner-occupied,

those tiny balls, domestic
as tea cosies, intricate

as an Arraiolos weave,
virtual houses, never

to be hatched in, in the bramble
perhaps, or the cork oak or laurel,

poems perfected
but never read,

does he revisit them, imagining other lives
he might have invented with different wives?

Old Sonnet

We stop at Adão, the smith's workshop.
Our arches shine in the gloom, awaiting
only a protective coat, and so shaped
and proportioned I seriously debate
abandoning our purple tunnel of grapes
and allowing his wrought-iron art
to soar and descend on its own terms. As I grip
his oily, metallic palm, he repeats
what I can deduce for myself, the trope
of stress and strain as opposites.
Each is precisely what I'd dared to hope,
as strict and radiant as an old sonnet,
and, of course, vines must do their duty,
completing purpose, re-doubling beauty.

Neighbours

Amadeu, on a plot no bigger than ours,
plants turnips in autumn and potatoes in spring.
He has geese, poultry, two cows and a goat,
with lemon and orange trees, a walnut and hazel,
pumpkins, a turquoise patch of cabbages,
and some carp in a tank fed by our watercourse.
On these riches, which he and his barrel-shaped wife
survey daily in stately perambulation, they
seem to prosper (though it leaves me wondering
who the devil he deals with for his bread and wine?).

Maria António, he of the lead-lined stomach
uncorroded by whatever drip-feeds our well,
owns the forest and a road-side allotment.
The forest's off-limits for planting. He forages
firewood, chestnuts, the odd rabbit or pigeon
with mushrooms and bay for the hunter's pot.
His allotment's resource is the moulded clay
for the miniature windmills with calico sails
he markets to passing tourists. Entrepreneur,
he knows his value, and of his kind, as decor.

Of the three, Anastásio most resembles us.
He has a van and descends unpredictably
with a kit like a diver's lungs, and insecto-
fungicide for his acre of vines. "The silkworms
and quails take most," he grumbles (or so
says my dictionary for what's more mundane).
But he does it from yearning, having another
life, other manoeuvres for securing his petrol,
his poisons, his satisfactions and his crust. It
makes us accomplices. He's the one I mistrust.

Trees

1

Cork oak, native to the Alentejo, a sort of
Irish-joke tree, yielding by way of pillage
not nuts nor sugar, but its very bark

in a below-the-waist striptease – an affair
of double negatives, as Lisbon humour has it.
You see them half-naked, their black

or mahogany bold as paintwork, each rising
from the pool of its own shadow
on the dry plain rolling to the Spanish border.

Southey, not the most nimble of poets,
thought cork oaks the loveliest trees of all.
Unfarmed, on the slopes of Sintra mounain

or in the natural forest of Monchique,
they turn pure gothic, harbouring creepers,
orchids, bats, and old lichens in fantastic

silhouettes, their masks furrowed as old
Auden's. A poet's tree, then, faintly
absurd, and most so when commercial,

– like the Alentejo peasants who
crop but don't own them, so
married to their hats they won't

enter a church, and anciently without
substitute for sealing the distillation of each
autumn on autumn's vintage.

2

Bluegums (*Eucalypti Globali*) aren't
liked here. They leach the soil,
bequeathing dustbowls. They're

commercial, compounding profit
in a mere ten years, something no
self-respecting tree should do. They uphold

concrete on ten thousand building sites,
Globalus being, like the builders themselves,
immigrant. Yet you'd never know

from its on-camera speed of growth
how tough this wood is. Creosoted,
it'll choke your drill, and a two-handed

frame-saw's needed to bring one to logs.
A graceful tree, tall as a poplar,
slender as a birch, its foliage

silver fish in a noon of August heat.
At the marginale turn-off,
an ancient ex-pat, a century young,

can be scented at 50 metres,
twice that after rain, its camphor
easing the fevers of the whole *bairro*.

3

Vine root's a twenty foot black
mamba fossilised in its writhing,

its knots untieable, its grip defying
earth-movers – for which

the two hundred year olive bole's
a mere ninety seconds yank. Across

bulldozed vineyards, they shoot
lime-fresh each April

as if the mechanical dinosaur
were an elaborate pruning hook.

Nothing we take in draws on deeper
arteries than grape vines, yielding

Ogun, Christ, and Dionysius,
so the most charitable,

murderous, inspired drunk's
in league with something of himself.

4

Then there's the religious orthodoxies
of the olive oil presses, viz.,

'ten per cent virgin', or better
'seven per cent extra', that

first odourless ooze without a menstrual trace of green
(but how can three per cent be purer than the ten?

degrees of virginity
more baffling than the Trinity).

I love the taste of olives
with their maculate, Arab flavour

and I like the stubbornness of olive trees,
the light that flashes from their metal leaves

like the mercury fountain in the Alhambra,
or the Cordoba

mosque with its bright logic
– viz., the most sacred relic

in old Glastonbury was a section
of the hole in which Christ's

tree stood. Holy, holey,
wholly, Lord God Almighty,

'gaze on this reliquary,
which is only apparently empty'

(and had they ninety-per-cent
or the infinitely purer ten?)

St Thomas with your loving doubt,
among the disciples, you were the poet!

Water

This long summer with the oily tips
of lemon trees curling like copper shavings,
I'm getting to know our *poço*

well. As the valley turns sepia,
and olive trees sharpen their knives,
and the blue gums are shoals of silver fish,

I draw on its quick secrets. At noon,
the shutter thrown back, sunlight
arrows down the green whitewash

to a shimmering, infinitely
beckoning circle and beyond
to water snake flashes in an abyss

impossible to climb from.
To subsist attuned to a well,
watching the trees breath, drinking

in bird song's a throwback
to develop, so
picture me, with my native off-spin,

bowling a plastic bucket to shatter
my face framed in the mirrored
hatch and haul miracle

draughts earthwards, well
aware if it doesn't flow,
I'm not working hard enough.

A Kind of Failure

That rarest of intellectual things
a wedding invitation,
Johnny and Jo, their beyond-
hope parents hoping
they'll indeed make a go
of it, the more lavish
the wedding, the more
binding the superglue;
so the bride's a cake
in her layers of icing,
with sugarplum attendants,
her groom the regulation
black-handled knife.

My son, my daughter,
if I bequeath you anything
as you try to buck the market,
my prayer is you negotiate
the difficult art of love,
knowing the voices against
are stronger than ever,
and a surviving marriage
is a kind of failure
(what's lacking in her
that she's happy with him,
what slavish devotion
is he basking in?).

At Ana and Paulo's,
even the priest, ebullient
in his jeans and surplice,
even the hippy priest, pulling

metaphors from the ropes
and anchor stonework
of his 500 year old
chapel, said: marriage
is like the *Carreira da India*;
of four carracks, risking
the Atlantic's winds and shoals,
only one returns cradling
rubies and peppers.

Voyaging is truly an aspect
of it, as are partner, lover,
passionate friend, live-in
helpmate, all the honourable
trite euphemisms that
yearn to reinvent love
and abolish property
in each other – appalled
by the flunky dictating
to the banquet hall,
hall of Ascot hats
and hired penguins, *Be
Upstanding for the Bride*

in the macabre ante-chamber
of an English nuptial. Yet beyond
the *Country Life* position,
the vomit on the en suite
carpet, the jetlagged
honeymoon, our prayer,
Jo and Johnny, is
you find anchorage

in each other. May you
live to discover (like
the Tswana for whom only
lifetimes are short enough
to consummate a marriage),

the enduring words for your
voluntary roping are
indeed 'wife' and 'husband'.
So let the skies rain
lark song from high
above the Quantocks,
and may the polluted
Severn be salmon-thronged,
then your estuary view
of Atlantic winds and shoals
will be only the normal
vicissitudes of lives
pregnant with happiness.

Literary Remains

Vasco's used to the latest custom,
but his father was appalled when
between the lying-in and the burial
the corpse was abandoned overnight.

'Overnight? In England, it's frozen
in the morgue till the family
drifts in from wherever with time
off work, maybe ten days or more.'

Now it's Vasco's scandalised. But he
has a grim duty. Here, the buried enjoy
a five year tenure before the bones
are lifted and boxed in the vault,

this resurrection needing a family
member present in law to approve
– his aunt, for instance, so embalmed
by her pills she took seven years

to qualify for the skeleton cupboard.
Babies, says Vasco, disturb him most
with their tiny rosaries and bird-like
ribs, and I yield him the palm

in this tournament of the macabre,
he being half my age in a matter ever
closer to the bone, and I far from re-
hearsed in my curtain-line rattle.

The Ethiopian Woman

When ageing Moses took as his umpteenth wife
the Ethiopian woman,

Aaron and his own wife Miriam
howled the tabernacle down.

So God descended in a pillar of thunder:
Moses was a true prophet, his word

was HIS word, and when the holy tornado
dispersed, Miriam found herself a leper.

Even Moses (there's an insert here,
claiming he was the mildest of men) even

he balked at this crime against humanity.
Caught in his prevarications, God

modified the sentence. If a man
spat in his wife's face, she was banned

from the camp seven days and nights. So
a restored Miriam served a week's exile,

all this in the Sinai, while the chosen people
were pining for those wet cucumbers

and Egypt's staff-of-life garlic. No one
comes well out of this tale, not

Moses with his tented master bedroom, nor
those proto-Afrikaners with their mixed-marriages

cant, nor God, a petulant Hastings Banda,
with his paraphernalia of magic.

Only the Ethiopian, her silences
silenced, lives in cultured rebuke.

Roman Style

The scythe's discarded blade with its gap tooth
rusts on the veranda. Spring's flowers
are levelled, the field's pared

to contours the swallows shave unerringly.
Our feeling's of summer no sooner come
than gone, but I never cease marvelling

about the seasons here, how harvest's
but a prelude to Julho and Agosto,
Roman inserted months, when the sun

scours like a blow torch, and our resort's
once more to our well-spring. It's not
what we are at heart feels different,

perhaps a little heavier, somewhat
slower to the beach ball, while judges,
presidents, even golfers, are ever younger,

and no TV adverts target us in their mooning
mock-Hollywood, thank god, for jeans
or face creams or exercise contraptions

as friends are crossing into the dark,
and it touches family ever closer. So,
the hatch sealed, we've sized up the well

with a pump buoy, and regale nightly
all we've planted with more than ever
loving and lavish draughts, hoping

Roman-fashion to insure against
something when the scythe rounds
on its owner and the plot lies bare.

A Different Valley

(after Virgil's 1st Eclogue)

Luís

Taliesin (what kind of name's that?), I watch you scribbling
there on your veranda with your sandals on that tiled table
glorying in your grapes and peppers, your apples and walnuts,
while I'm being evicted from this fertile valley I've
known every inch of since before I learned my catechism.
I'm expelled from my fields with my goats and my ancient wife
to put up with my daughter in the next town, while you loll
in leafy shade, pretending to pretend your trees and flowers
come together in praising your 'beautiful Carapinha'.

Taliesin

Luís, it's Welsh, and I've a patron, a young fogy in a suit
who likes to practise his English. So long as I make him
monthly offerings, he gives me ample freedom to compose.

Luís

I don't grudge any man his freedom, but I have to tell you
this could never have happened under the dictatorship! I should
have checked my *Borda d'Agua* when that lightning bolt
struck the cork oak in my yard. Look, my pet she-goat
can hardly move. She dropped her twins on builders' rubble
in the shadow of a concrete wall, where I remember olive trees
and a perennial stream. Now my landlord wants my cottage
and allotment to re-develop as a petrol station. But tell me
about this lord of yours. Who is he with all his largesse?

Taliesin

That city you call Lisboa, there on the Tagus – in my folly
I thought it a city of squares and funiculars and pavement
cafes, a quiet retreat from empire, where the best food by far

is by far the cheapest. Yet these days with the euro, I kid
you not, Lisbon's a great place for every kind of business.

Luís

So what brought you to Portugal? What was the temptation?

Taliesin

Has she a name, the Goddess of travel? I spent decades
in her service, jet-zagging oceans you bold Lusitanians
were the first ever to map. Whatever money I made,
I spent in her cause, that ripe-breasted anonymous one
who hides below the horizon. But all this time, my alert
Carapinha was at my side, and at last I respected her counsel.

Luís

I used to wonder what family feuds left the land you occupy
abandoned. Grapes soured on vines run wild, apples
rotted on the unmown grass, and the thousand year old
watercourse I drank from hunting sparrows as a boy, all
shouted for someone to unblock and harrow and prune.

Taliesin

What was I to do? She found the land yearning, and it matched
a need in ourselves. I tracked down my silk-tied fogy
with a bank to make profitable and mortgages on offer.
Twelve times a year my account bleeds, and in this fifth
age of my manhood, he lets me pretend I'm a farmer.

Luís

You lucky cuckolder! So a mortgage grants title to what's
not truly yours? Well, you're free to enjoy our dispossession.
It's not the most fertile land, no long-abandoned vineyard

is, but it's well-watered. The apple and pear trees cast
cool, rotating shadows. You can line up your hives
where the *canna* glows in the sunset, and no swallows
will swoop to catch the returning bees. Your arched
vines will yield you ample wine, your she-goats the ripest
cheeses. Take your olives to Diogo's press, and your corn
to be stone-ground in Pedro's windmill. Otherwise, you
need no one, save your lovely Carapinha, with her chickens
and her pigeon house, and the flowers she likes to fill
your house with. I admit I never planted flowers in my life.

Taliesin

Sooner shall Greeks and Turks mingle across
their common frontier to share each other's wives, than
I'll regret my encounter with that entrepreneur in a suit.

Luís

But we others must pack up, like those east Europeans
migrating here, we must scatter where there's employment,
to England, serving from menus that appal us, to Germany
fighting Turks for a wage below the minimum, or home
to Africa to run some bottle store, though that's risky
business, for our old skills aren't respected. No point being
homesick. Childhood's a different valley, made alien
by *novos ricos* who never milked a she-goat, or rubbed
well-tilled soil between thumb and fingertips. No more
shepherding for me. To such a pass has the revolution
brought us!

Taliesin

Luís, you're welcome to spend this night as our guest. We've
a Welsh roast with apple and chestnut sauce, and robust

Torres Vedras wines along with an active cheese. Look,
the sun's sinking. The pine trees' shadows have doubled.
Smoke is furling from the first of this winter's hearth fires.

Trees again

Around where I now have purchase
are so many abandoned trees,

once integral to the small farms'
hoe-to-mouth economies,

orphaned by the developers
who move in with their bulldozers

and I wish I could adopt them.

The mossy dry-stone walls,
the water-courses and the wells,

the donkey tracks, the sheep pens,
are rubble in an afternoon,

but the odd tree on the computer-
mapped Byron Village print-out

is allowed (heavily lopped

and transplanted) a stunted heritage
as architect's camouflage

for the lack of virtue in what's deflowering
what was here before,

and I wish I could adopt them.

The Platform

John's 19th birthday barbecue
the week before they both depart.
The platform by the old plum tree
that once hurled me to the ground's
yet to be tiled, but no matter.
There's the sound of running water
and a concrete base for tables and chairs,
the charcoal's already tinkling,
and for the first time we can see the spot
Alice chose gets the last of the sunset.

'Haven't you got a light down here?'
says Francisco, protesting the obvious.
By the time the spare ribs are done
it's starlight, and the peppered chicken's
served blindfold but delicious.
There's a good wine and cold beer,
we huddle in the slight chill,
and Alex indulges to the full
his drinking half and opening another,
as we toast John and celebrate his brother.

The looming wall of invisible canna's
a jagged tear at the sky's edge;
to the west, pines are silhouetted,
and revolving above us, in this
breeze from the furrowed Atlantic,
this out-of-town blackness, are
Orion and the Great Bear,
the Plough and distant Pleiades,
conspiring with the hour hand
that returns our sons to England.

I confide to Alice, 'We create
the stage on which they play out
their departures, nothing more.'
But for her, land, ancestors
and inheritance are not oases
on a desert journey, but
the beginning and purposed end.
Each shared meal, every heeled-in
root is like the northern star: a lantern,
a fixity, a magnet, and a legend.

I remember the exodus and the psalms,
the antipodes of my childhood:
the straight and narrow pilgrimage,
the annual round of milk and honey.
Like it or not, they are on their way
and their visits will be seasonal,
Christmas, and familial summer,
as the other loyalties we pray
will be theirs exert their tidal pull,
delivering other ceremonies of survival.

Fado

When Vasco da Gama captained Benfica,
those were the glory days. Vasco led
from the back, with Nick Coelho as keeper,
and his brother Paulo as inside-forward,

and Leonard Ribeira, an old-fashioned winger
(except when eyeing the girls in the crowd),
and the sprinter Fernão Veloso as striker,
with Diogo and Álvaro, all proud to wear red.

Those were the times of adventure and clout,
with Dom Manoel our manager-trainer
and Peru de Covilhã our roving scout.

Today we're trophy-less, bankrupt and disdained,
longing for Sebastian, cresting some tidal wave
on his surf-board, to alight in the Algarve.

Dry Stone Walls

Two channel streams, the third secures
the two-metre precipice to the forest
boundaries. When a stone here
before the language I use existed is
dislodged, it's mere ritual to replace it.

There's rhythm in dry stone walls,
mineral shifts from crystal to ochre,
to turquoise and scarlet in the toe-hold
plantlings, the mosses and lichens,
each minute and back from sunlight to cloud.

Yet thistledown invades and bees plunder
unprosecuted. Our snake ignores
the watercourse boulders that suck
its bootlace in, and swallows
are untrammelled in their private creole

of clicks and screams. I love old walls,
I admire wall breachers. I condemn
new walls. I thrive on privacy.
There's no resolving this conundrum
as the sound of water sculpting stones

blends with the piping of hatched
martins, a blessing on our eaves.
All histories, all beliefs take off
somewhere from this image, building
their subtle, self-validating systems.

It all turns on the four elements:
shelter, partnership, offspring,

and the possibilities of story. Within
these walls, there's living to be done.
After the house, there's still the travelling on.

Loners

In this late summer Atlantic mist a lone
swallow circles. Its twists and plummeting
are inventive as ever, but somehow
irresolute. It has the look of one
about to depart, before bats

take over the lengthening dusks, and cicadas
return to their shrilling. Swallows, beyond
all else in nature, have worked out
how to live. They mob the gothic tower, milling
like termites round the sunlit tiles as we watch

from the square in shadow. Above the weir,
they scud through the roman bridge marking tiny v.s
in the stonework's reflection. They
never cower, they're not landlocked, their
rationale is warmth. Once

I saw an albino swallow, hurtling
into the sunset like a spun tile. It
peaked like an asterisk in the emerging dome,
and I imagined, lone freak, him tracking
earth's magnetic index, crossing

the Sahara like the Wise Men's star.

Affinity

The afternoon we crush
the last of the yellowing
basil feels of all summer's
endings, the last.

I've written little
about endings, though
the three or four women
I broke with, I think of at times.

Women are, for the most part,
what it's been about,

and though I'm long past twice the age
I made my final choice
and was chosen,
how much better not
to have done harm and been harmed.

'The herb' (Culpepper, 1653)
'which all authors are together
by the ears about'.

Let's celebrate its redolent oils,
its special affinity with tomatoes.

Some Silicon Heaven

(for António Rui, d. July 2002)

1

An African grief, with its harrowing
rituals, its staged spontaneity, its
strictly ordered wailing, the men
stern-faced, the women
out of control, yet
queuing for their moment, while

beyond all in the cramped apartment,
the TV crooning, the hi-fi
on maximum, as though here
in Lisbon, far from
likuba drums and the ecstasy
of dancing, something

rhythmic and cacophonous
has to be hurled in death's
maw – though Rui of all men
would have welcomed
professionally his obsequies'
punctuation by mobile phones...

2

Some lower the dead
into the earth;
the final instinct is growth.

Some place the dead
on funeral pyres,
fire to ash and fertiliser.

The truest burial's
at sea, all at sea,
salt tears, inconsolable.

3

The burial was simple, the coffin
opened at the graveside for final
cold kisses, then plunged no more
than a metre down, divided by less
than half that from the fresh grave
to the left (n° 548), and from the first
of five holes to the right, awaiting
the corpses queuing up behind us.

A plain ceremony in the municipal
cemetery at the municipality's
expense. Grim to leave Rui so
close to the surface, "in sure and certain
hope of the resurrection". The priest
strode quickly away, his robe flapping.

4

Rui, born in the *bairro*, father unknown,
with a cleft palate, a game leg, and sores
corrupting his eardrums,

would hobble the tracks between tin-roofed shanties
where women sweated at mortars or dragged behind them
huge water barrels,

with a watch strapped to his left wrist, a transistor
clapped to his right ear, gold teeth smiling, his shades
reflecting coconut palms,

and jabbering, stammering in tortured Portuguese
of a Grundig next year, a Suzuki, an outboard motor,
a Boeing 707 to Lisbon,

and we shared the joke. What worked and gleamed
he worshipped. People being flawed irreparably,
gadgets were his ikons.

5

So the censored version of what I published
years back, in the glee of discovering
he'd made it to the Grundig and Lisbon
being 'voluble with images as ever'. But

'his township mother' who was 'always,
grinned the white managers, available
if you were desperate,' is before me now
in the desperation of her grief, the one

lady left here Alice can speak with
in her mother tongue, and I feel shame
at something that teases and eludes.
Nothing I wrote was untrue, in praises

to celebrate his arrival. But Death
the Leveller promotes, and Rui's

departure chastens. He was
so sure he'd made it, absconding

from the girl he'd made pregnant
all those years back in Marromeu,
to the cramped ring of social
housing, and his '*mulher da terra*'.

Our friendship stood on the fallible
premise he amply reciprocated,
that his life was one long joke.
I've other friends who say this,

none who lived the part so fully.
Now his narrow cell imposes
its strictures, and I wonder
by what right I become his poet,

some ambivalent means of getting out
being all I ever contributed
to the countries I tried to help,
and he secured that without me.

More fitting the albums of sepia
photos, the annual masses sung
to a god he loved to ridicule,
the municipal headstone, the videos

with their countless, milling extras,
that extended, unregistered family
cramped in the box his widow
inherits the common-law right

to occupy; these are his legacy,
more than any words of mine;
penned in by the truth he will
never again be uncontainable Rui.

6

In my sober dream, the motorway
continued. I had missed the turn-off,
then all turn-offs ceased, with all

road signs, petrol stations, cafes,
toll booths, just the concrete
rolling onwards through a misty

countryside with a brimming river,
and huge trucks and pantechnicons
racing both ways, three abreast

on the dizzying five chain curves
but never colliding, just waltzing
marvellously, free as skylarks

from the five senses and motion's
laws, and the dear lately dead
driving, wholly with us, uncorrupted.

7

So uncoffin him, let's celebrate his life!
He'd nothing, yet what he made of it beggared
all I have to offer.

Books, career, responsibility, investment, none
stretched so far as his world. Cable
TV did,

but only as a shining, channel-hopping box.
No programme, not even football, ever gagged
his flow of commentary.

With invention, he suffered no handicap.
A poet, then, re-claiming the world,
with the knack

to impose his dialect, in answering
which unwittingly all of us mimicked
his impediment.

We never quitted his stall without
indulging his newest rhapsody
of a Concord flight

to some silicon heaven where the latest-
bred clones have interchangeable
body parts.

So invent on, my dear dead friend,
in the lives of those you gave ballast to,
and count me in.

By the River Taff

Killing time by the River Taff
six decades on in a park
of daffodils, I relive
my earliest memory.
What, before I was three,
taught me to pick
up a stone and loop it half
way across this same pewter stream
as I mimic now in a kind of dream?

A child, a stone, a river,
the river, a stone, a pensioner,
yet I feel no different:
travel, career, our jade wedding,
any shore with pebbles, my instinct's
still to chuck one in;
and though knowledge elects
to make one skip six or eight
before it plunges, it seems precious little.

The river descends, the stone's
polished to sculpture.
In this century of winged
heels, I've a reading
to do and a plane
to catch, as old choices
sweep me on. My trade's
casting poems to the stream,
though the histories that grab me

have always been other peoples'.
That three year old

who looped the pebble,
fascinates as some foreigner
what impelled him, etc?
– yet I've borne
him within me, like a foetus
long maturing, the child
the man's grandfather, *amen*.

Suddenly, there's a new noise in my life

with a different rhythm.

It comes from the soak-away under the pine trees
beyond the stone wall in Pasqual's plot,
and it's called croaking, though

no sound's more bullish, more pulsing with semen than this
throaty chuck chuckle, this guttural
rasping on a rising fifth, swelling at the larynx
like a condom, and ending in a whoop.

I'm coming to know Pasqual's frogs,
like we know our individual wren.

That's Kermit, we say at first light
with his oink oink and purring whistle,
then Baron Scarpia abandons snoring
for his bass bassoon and kettle drum
to the wren's sweet piccolo,
a surer reveille than Amadeu's rooster
hallooing half the night.

Croaking, is it? I'll show you croaking.
From my wheelchair by the kitchen door
when whatever it is
is no longer operable,
I'll grunt my poems, *Vissi d'arte*,
while Pasqual's frogs supply the treble.

On the Run

This wren, this half-sparrow
with no neck, its tail stuck on

like a feather in the cap,
has commandeered our veranda,

startling us from sleep
with its trills and warbling, a looping whistle,
                                        and nine rounds of rapid chatter.

I draw the curtain an inch, and it's there,
chest tight as a ping-pong ball, lower beak rigid,

then a quick fire vibrato with oscillating shrills,
tail quivering like a baton

as it boasts to the valley,
This is my territory.

We know it from all the other wrens in the orchard.
That's ours, we say, no need to look round

from sowing onions or watering the lily bed.
This wren has us on the run.

From the day it first intruded
with a beakful of lichen,

the chairs, the flowerpots,
the tiled table where I draft my poems,

have been strictly off-limits,
as this womb-shaped nest incubating

the tiniest of the frailest
has us fretting, after

Freddie, Jean and George gone,
why we feel so chosen,

why in heaven would it matter
so much if he let us scare them off.

Thursday Market

"A man should know how to skin a rabbit" (Orwell)

These days I catch myself telling
friends, 'Those pheasants I plucked
had olives in their crops
and olive stones in their gizzards,'

which for me was an epiphany,
for though the baby-smooth olives
vanished singly from the sapling
John bought at Thursday market

(and was questioned *What an oliveira!*
Where will you plant it? Are those
your parents? Mozambique? Wales?
What a lovely oliveira! every

metre he shouldered it to the car park),
I never saw game birds gorging
on those astringent beads, those goat
droppings, that uncured olives are.

There's mysteries at Thursday
market, not the cell phones, or oils
of Our Lady, or the skimpy
knickers spread-eagled on cardboard,

but gadgets of no apparent use
– like the aluminum tub, with a cup
to one side and a sliding blade
below and above a two-inch hole:

(you bucket a chicken, with its comb
through the hole, and guillotine it,

catching the blood for a *cabidela*
all the farmers here swear by);

for the more I pursue this business
of getting in touch with neighbours
who in their turn appear more in touch
with the planet that sustains us,

the further I seem to be drifting
from friends I admire, but who buy
their nut roasts cellophane wrapped
and never skinned a rabbit in their lives.

Against Reflection

The first time the rioting peasants
stormed into the Governor's
ivory palace, they stopped short
at the full-length looking-glass. Never
before, in forest pools or the missionaries'
mirrors, had they seen themselves
whole, red-eyed, with cow dung braids,
their pangas menacing their reflection.

Me, for example, my glinting panga
curving to the shins of this *canna*,
wellies, pants, torn shirt, disdaining
levis or shades or a straw hat, as
each professional day I scorn
tie and briefcase, in my refraction
of classlessness. Once mirrors
enter your life, there's no end to it.

Mimesis: imita-making, of course,
but the props of what's worth
inventing shift. We are in a garden,
more precisely, a garden in a poem.
Not that I'm cheating, it really exists
out there, beyond the arches,
I could show you around with pride
and pleasure, pointing out...

but here's the argument. Having
indicated the garlic bed need
I, now it's in the poem's mirror,
bother watering it next day?
The book about the garden's

done, my latest re-baptism,
and the house, the authentic
metaphor of her who designed it.

Narcissus, Echo's toy boy,
pined away in self contemplation,
and she, too, faded, so that
all that survived was a cadence.
Something has root in me that
longs to shatter the looking-glass
to somewhere aboriginal, as at last
in middle age I turn romantic...

Morning Glory

Morning Glory dawns china blue
and all day following the sun
subtly changes register,
going out in a blaze of purple,

and every morning, May to November,
unfailingly there are fresh blossoms
following the same course,
sky blue to the original bougainvillea,

a day's life from the colour of ice
to the colour of the pine tree's long shadow
on the pantile earth of summer:
I'm glad I recorded this.

Acknowledgements

Acknowledgements are due to the editors of *Moving Worlds*, *Poetry Wales* and *Where the Angolans are Playing Football: Selected and New Poetry* (Parthian, 2003) where some of these poems first appeared.